# How To Make Your First $1,000 With Online Surveys

By Chris Guthrie

http://ChrisGuthrieBooks.com

Text copyright © 2014 Chris Guthrie
All Rights Reserved

## Disclaimer and Terms of Use

DISCLAIMER AND TERMS OF USE AGREEMENT

The author and publisher of this book and the accompanying materials have used their best efforts in preparing this book. The author and publisher make no representation or warranties with respect to the accuracy, applicability, fitness, or completeness of the contents of this book. The information contained in this book is strictly for informational purposes. Therefore, if you wish to apply ideas contained in this book, you are taking full responsibility for your actions.

Every effort has been made to accurately represent this book and it's potential. Even though this industry is one of the few where one can write their own check in terms of earnings, there is no guarantee that you will earn any money using the techniques and ideas in these materials. Examples in these materials are not to be interpreted as a promise or guarantee of earnings. Earning potential is entirely dependent on the person using our book, ideas and techniques. We do not purport this as a "get rich scheme." any claims made of actual earnings or examples of actual results can be verified upon request. Your level of success in attaining the results claimed in our materials depends on the time you devote to the knowledge and various skills. Since these factors differ according to individuals, we cannot guarantee your success or income level. Nor are we responsible for any of your actions

Materials in our product and our website may contain information that includes or is based upon forward-looking statements within the meaning of the Securities Litigation Reform Act of 1995. Forward-looking statements give our expectations or forecasts of future events. You can identify these statements by the fact that they do not relate strictly to historical or current facts. They use words such as "anticipate," "estimate," "expect," "project," "intend," "plan," "believe," and other words and terms of similar meaning in connection with a description of potential earnings or financial performance.

Any and all forward looking statements here or on any of our sales material are intended to express our opinion of earnings potential. Many factors will be important in determining your actual results and no guarantees are made that you will achieve results similar to ours or anybody else's. In fact, no guarantees are made that you will achieve any results from our ideas and techniques in our material.

The author and publisher disclaim any warranties (express or implied), merchantability, or fitness for any particular purpose. The author and publisher shall in no event be held liable to any party for any direct, indirect, punitive, special, incidental or other consequential damages arising directly or indirectly from any use of this material, which is provided "as is" and without warranties.

As always, the advice of a competent legal, tax, accounting, or other professional should be sought.

The author and publisher do not warrant the performance, effectiveness, or applicability of any sites listed or linked to in this book.

All links are for information purposes only and are not warranted for content, accuracy, or any other implied or explicit purpose.

## Table of Contents:

Your Free Book Bonus: 50+ Legitimate Survey Websites
What You Can Expect to Learn from This Book
Can You Really Make Money Taking Surveys Online?
How to Avoid Scams When Taking Online Surveys
Why Some Legitimate Survey Sites Are Better Than Others
The Various Ways to Make Money with These Sites
Survey Routers
Survey Taking Ethics
General Survey Taking Tips
The Best Survey Sites and How to Use Them
Swagbucks
CashCrate
iPoll
Ipsos i-Say
Opinion Outpost
SurveySpot
Paid Viewpoint
MindSwarms
InboxDollars
BzzAgent
How to Best Combine All the Survey Companies
Final Impressions on Taking Surveys for Money
Thank You

# Your Free Book Bonus: 50+ Legitimate Survey Websites

While the information in this book is more than enough to set you on the path to making your first $1,000 with online survey companies, I want to give you some bonus material as appreciation for purchasing this book.

**Here is a list of over 50+ legitimate survey websites**:

http://ChrisGuthrieBooks.com/bonus-websites

I've attempted or researched each of these websites on my quest to review every single survey company. Enjoy the rest of this book and thank you again for taking the time to read it.

# What You Can Expect to Learn from This Book

Hello! My name is Chris Guthrie, and I currently generate a growing six figure income from various online businesses and activities. I've tried a lot of survey companies to test this method of earning money online, so I'm excited to share with you what I've learned so you can get started right away.

In this book, you can expect to learn why companies are willing to pay you to take surveys, how to avoid online scams, the various ways to make money with these companies, survey tips (such as paying taxes on your earnings), and how to make the most money in the shortest amount of time.

However, the best part of this book, and the part that will help you the most, is where I reveal to you my top survey taking companies, and exactly how to **make the most money with them for the least amount of time**. This section of the book will save you tons of time and headache, since I have personally found and tested these gems of sites.

If you follow the strategies and recommendations in this book, you will be well on your way to making your first $1,000 with online survey companies. I will teach you exactly how to add a decent amount of money to your monthly income, all from your computer.

# Can You Really Make Money Taking Surveys Online?

When people initially think about making money with online surveys, the first thought that comes to mind is "scam." This is completely understandable, as most people don't realize how valuable their opinion actually is.

Survey sites are actually websites that are run by market research firms in order to get information for their clients. Market research firms do exactly what their name implies - they research markets. Specifically, markets of distinct demographics, such as a 30-year-old white male with children, or a 60-year-old female from Canada.

The survey sites, called survey panels, are how the market research companies collect their information. The information they collect from you is used towards things such as identifying the potential for a new product or service, getting feedback on an existing product, or your thoughts on current events and political topics. There are many reasons why they want your opinion.

**The best part is that they are willing to pay you for it.**

Market research firms know that filling out surveys is not something that people would want to do for free, so they give the survey participants rewards for completing surveys. This is why you can make money from survey sites, and learning how to do so will allow you to get **the most money in the least amount of time**.

Making money from these survey sites seems very straight forward, and it is, *if you know which companies are legitimate and how to best use them*. This is where things get complicated. Since it is very easy to build out websites and pretend to be a legitimate survey panel website, you have to be careful to avoid scam websites.

This is why I've created this book, and why I run SurveyChris.com, my survey panel review website.

## How to Avoid Scams When Taking Online Surveys

Unfortunately, there are scam websites all over the Internet. Without the correct knowledge, it is very easy to fall victim to these scams. The first tip I have to avoid scams is to simply follow the directions here in this book. The websites and strategies I layout are tested and focus only on legitimate sites.

However, if you would like to know how I personally avoid being scammed, I have a few rules that I follow for survey sites.

**Rule #1:** Never pay to join a survey panel. These survey panels should be paying you. Not the other way around.

**Rule #2:** Check to see if a market research firm runs the company. Then do research on the market research firm. Their BBB profile is a good place to start.

**Rule #3:** Look for contact information on the survey site. All good survey sites will have a way for you to contact them.

**Rule #4:** Look at what information the survey sites are looking for. No legitimate survey site will ask for your Social Security number, bank account information, or passwords.

**Rule #5:** Look for honest reviews from *actual* members of these sites. My website is a good place to start for that, since I join, use, and attempt to cash out with each survey site I review.

While it is a good idea to keep those five rules in mind when looking at survey sites, I have done so when reviewing the sites in this book and on my website so that you can focus on making money.

In later sections of this book I'll also give you tips on **how to avoid getting your personal email inbox spammed** with thousands of emails, and **how to avoid the unsolicited calls to your phone**.

While avoiding scams and using legitimate sites is the first step towards making money with survey sites, it is not enough. Later, I will cover why some legitimate sites are better than others, and later on in the book, I will show you exactly which ones you should be using, and how to exactly use them to get the most money for your time.

# Why Some Legitimate Survey Sites are Better than Others

Finding legitimate survey sites is a major step towards making your first $1,000 with survey sites, but it is not nearly enough. To reach that kind of money, you need to not only be using legitimate sites, but you need to be using the *right* legitimate paying websites.

### Highest Payout for Least Amount of Time

The right survey taking websites are the ones that have **the highest payouts for the least amount of time spent**. These websites won't get you rich over night, but if you use them consistently, you will start to see good money coming in.

There are certain requirements that I have when looking for the best sites. Some of the best sites I've found can pay out around $10 an hour, but your results may differ. Again as I've said before this isn't a get rich quick method but it is a surefire way of making at least some money online. (Later, I'll cover the various ways to make money with these sites).

### Surveys Tailored to the User

Another factor I take into consideration is that some companies are better at sending surveys to you that you are more likely to qualify for. I'm not sure why some companies are better at this than others, but from my experience, there is a difference in each company. I want companies that send me surveys tailored towards my demographic, based on past surveys and profiles I have filled out.

### Loyalty and Bonus Programs

I also look for sites with loyalty bonuses. Only a couple sites offer this, and they are some of my favorites. I enjoy loyalty bonuses, because it is **basically free money**. I would already be using these sites, so to be rewarded extra for doing so is a great plus.

### Getting Paid for Doing Something I Would Be Doing Anyways

Another factor that I take into play when looking for good survey sites to use is if they will pay me for something I would already be doing. Some sites pay for shopping online through their websites, or taking pictures and reviewing products while at the store. So if I'm going to do something already, I have a list of sites that I look through first.

For example, if I want to go to a restaurant, I typically check Groupon first to see if there is a deal. However, after discovering the best survey sites, I now look through Inbox Dollars, since **they give $5 for every $20 spent** on Groupons. There are options for coupons on survey sites for items that you probably buy all the time.

It is important to know that not all sites payout the same and offer the same activities to make money. The sites I list here in the book are the top notch sites, and using them will get you to your first $1,000 faster than using other sites. Especially when you use the tricks and tips I have for each site.

# The Various Ways to Make Money with These Sites

So while this book seems to be only about taking surveys online, there are actually tons of ways to make money through these survey websites. As I mentioned, some sites have better strengths than others, and I'll show you those in this book. For now, I'd like to cover the different ways you can make money with these sites, and explain how they work.

**Surveys**

First is the standard survey. This is as simple as it can get. You answer survey questions and get paid for them. The surveys vary in length and payment. But typically, you want to be earning at least $1 per 10 minutes on average. The sites I recommend will offer surveys around and above that amount.

**Offers**

A second way to make money through these sites is offers. This is slightly more complicated and is not typically run by market research firms. Some websites, including a couple that I recommend, have offers available through their dashboards. These are offers to sign up for websites or services. Some are free, and some cost money.

While "cost money" may raise an alarm, especially with spam in mind, this is actually my favorite way to make money with these websites. A paid offer typically involves buying a basic service, or getting a discounted service or product, and then getting paid for doing so. This involves some simple math, to make sure you are being paid more then you are spending.

I have made around **$5 multiple times for less than a minute of work** with these paid surveys. The good ones are as simple as signing up, recording when the free or discounted trial ends, and setting a reminder in your phone and/or calendar to cancel the service before the reoccurring payment begins. It honestly takes less than a minute to go through the entire process.

There are also free offers available, but they typically take longer and pay out less than paid offers. I will cover offers in more detail when I get to the sites that I recommend doing offers on.

**Product Testing**

Thirdly, and one of the most fun ways, is to become a product tester. Companies need feedback on their physical products, such as food items, clothing, and just about anything you can think of. To become a product tester, you simply sign up for product testing sites (I'll tell you the best one later), and you fill out profile surveys so they know your demographic.

You are not guaranteed to be sent a product right when signing up. Once a company wants to test a product with your demographic, you will be notified by email. You are then either able to accept or reject the invitation, then test the product if you do accept it. You then give them feedback or even help them generate buzz about their product if you like it enough.

**And Many More**

Lastly, there are a bunch of random ways to make money on these various sites that don't need much explanation. You can get paid for watching videos, playing games, using their search engines, clipping coupons from their sites, reading emails, taking polls and guessing trivia questions.

These tend to have lower payouts, and on some sites are completely not worth it. But when I go over the recommended sites and how to best use them, I'll show you the best way to take advantage of all the money making opportunities with these sites.

# Survey Routers

Once you are in the world of taking surveys online, you will definitely come across the term "survey routers." These are websites that you sign up for that send surveys directly to your email from the actual market research survey panels.

While this sounds convenient at first, it is not the ideal way to make money with taking surveys. The problem with survey routers is that it doesn't allow you to take advantage of tricks and tips that will get you the most money for your time.

They don't send you the highest paying activities, and you don't get access to some of the better features that come with actually joining the survey panels. Also, I have noticed that some survey routers charge you for their services. This either comes in the form of a sign up cost (remember, never pay to join survey panels or routers), or they take a little off the top of your survey rewards, so you get paid less.

In the end, it is better to join the survey companies yourself and keep track of where you need to go to take surveys and participate in activities. This will make you way more money in the end.

# Survey Taking Ethics

Before I get into the general survey tips section on how to best take surveys, I felt the need to touch on the ethics of taking surveys. While by all means I want you to get the most money for the least amount of time from these survey companies, I don't believe in giving false information or rushing through surveys to the point where you are not honestly answering the questions.

Some survey companies actually try to combat this type of behavior by putting in trick questions and contacting you if you are going through surveys at a speed that is unnatural.

Later, I will give you honest ways to do surveys quicker and make more money from them, but I don't support dishonest means of doing so. Market research companies truly want this information to improve the products, services, and policies you and I use on a daily basis.

There is a reason companies are willing to pay you for your opinion. They find it valuable and actually use it to make decisions. With that in mind, it is necessary to be honest on the surveys.

# General Survey Taking Tips

This chapter is where I will break down for you the best general survey taking tips. These will help you keep track of your surveys and survey companies, avoid getting your inbox flooded with emails, make money quicker, and strategies that work across the board when it comes to making money online with survey companies.

## Keeping Track of Your Surveys and Survey Companies

When it comes to making money with survey companies, it is best to sign up for multiple companies and constantly be working with each one. The reason for this is that these companies don't have an endless supply of surveys and ways for you to make money.

If you sign up with multiple companies, it will allow you to always have a way to make money available. Also, since different companies have different strengths and weaknesses, **combining these companies allows you to utilize their strengths while avoiding their weaknesses**.

An example of this is that iPoll has a high minimum payout at $50. However, they have a great mobile app, pay above industry standards for surveys, and have a decently high qualifying rate when it comes to surveys. Now if iPoll was the only site I was using, then I would get frustrated having to wait a longer time for every paycheck.

However, if you sign up for multiple companies, you will have checks coming in all the time from different survey companies. This way, you don't mind waiting longer for iPoll's payout because other companies are paying you out quicker.

One of the problems that comes with using multiple survey companies is that you sometimes forget which companies you have signed up for, which surveys you have taken, and how close you are to payouts.

For that reason, I have created this Excel sheet that you can download and fill out with every survey. It will make your life much easier when it comes to online surveys.

You can get my survey tracker by typing this into your brower:

http://surveychris.com/wp-content/uploads/2014/07/Survey-Tracker.xlsx

## Using a New Email Address Specifically for Surveys

One problem that is unavoidable with these survey companies and the offers they provide is getting your email spammed. This would be a major problem if you didn't know this trick I'm about to show you, which is to get **a second email address** and to save your personal inbox for, well, personal things.

This first method is my preferred one, but requires Gmail.

The first step is to get a secondary email. I personally use chris@surveychris.com to sign up for survey companies. If you don't have a secondary email to use, there is a simple solution.

If your email address is johndoe@gmail.com, then you could use the email address johndoe+surveys@gmail.com. The surveys that you use this address to sign up for will still come to johndoe@gmail.com, but if you use the "+surveys" label in the filtering system I'm about to show you, it will work the same as a secondary email.

So you now have a secondary email for surveys. Now you will want to filter every email sent to this survey email address into its own label within Gmail.

In Gmail, go to "Settings," then to the "Labels" tab, and scroll down to the "Labels" section and select "Create new label."

Here you will want to create a label called "Surveys." After the label is completed, switch over to your "Filters" section and set up a filter for your secondary email. In the options, make sure to check "Skip the Inbox (Archive)" and to apply the label you just created called "Surveys."

Then check "Never send it to Spam," to avoid losing surveys sent to you. This will unfortunately mean a lot of spam ends up in your "Surveys" filter, but it is necessary so that you don't lose your survey opportunities.

This is what my filter setup looks like:

To find your surveys in the filter, just look at your list of survey companies and search for them in the top search bar in Gmail.

This is how to set up a secondary email that you can access within your own Gmail account, while saving your primary inbox from spam. If you don't have Gmail, then another simple trick is to use a service such as Quick Inbox to create a disposable E-mail address.

I prefer using the filtering in Gmail, because of its convenience of already being connected to my personal Gmail account.

## How to Avoid Unsolicited Calls

Sometimes survey companies will ask for your phone number. While this is a way for companies to actually verify you as a real user, since they have to fight against scams as well, your number can sometimes make it onto public call records.

This can be extremely annoying if it is your home or cell phone number. This is where Google comes in handy again. I use a free Google Voice number for all of my surveys. Google Voice will translate and save all of my voicemails for me, so I don't have to deal with people calling my actual phone and listening through messages.

I recommend setting one up before you sign up for anything, as this will save your personal phone number.

## How to Never Lose an Account Password and Fill Out Forms Quicker

If you are signing up for multiple survey companies, you will have a ton of login information to remember: multiple usernames and multiple passwords. Luckily, there is a little piece of **free software** that completely eliminates this problem. It is called Last Pass.

Last Pass is a completely secure software and browser plugin that will generate and save passwords for you. You can then set it to automatically fill in the login information for you when you arrive at a website. This is extremely convenient, and will make sure that you aren't forgetting which password goes to what site.

Another great feature from Last Pass is that you can create profiles on it that you can use to **automatically fill in sign up forms**. You simply fill out one sign up form within Last Pass, then when you come across signup forms for survey companies or offers, you just click on the fill form option from Last Pass, and it instantly puts in your information.

This is particularly handy when it comes to filling out offers, as it makes it an extremely quick process, so you can **make money even faster**.

Another option is Roboform, which can save usernames and passwords and fill out forms similar to Last Pass. I personally use Last Pass, but both are good options.

### Always Fill Out Profile Surveys First

Most companies have what are called profile surveys. These surveys are available right when you sign up for an account. I recommend filling these out first every time (except with Swagbucks, as I'll explain in my Swagbucks section).

The reason these profile surveys are so important is that they narrow down your demographic, so the survey companies can send you surveys that you are more likely to qualify for. If the survey company knows nothing about you, then you have access to a large pool of surveys. This sounds good, but your qualifying rate for the surveys will be much lower, and **you will end up wasting a ton of time getting screened out of surveys.**

Save yourself the trouble and fill out the profile surveys. Sometimes, the survey companies will even pay you for filling these profile surveys out.

### Avoid Surveys that Don't Tell You Pay and Estimated Time

After you have signed up for survey companies and are actually taking the surveys, sometimes you will come across surveys, or entire survey panels, that don't tell you how much you will be paid for completing the survey and how long it will take.

I try to avoid these surveys. If I want to make the most money for my time, then I need to know how much I'm going to be paid and what the estimated time is. Based on my experience, about 95% of the time I am able to finish a survey at or below the estimated time. Now this will vary from survey panels and with different people, but I would guess most people have similar experiences.

The last thing I want to do is take a survey that I don't know anything about, and end up only making a few cents for a long time of working. Make sure you know the survey payout and the estimated time.

**Paying Taxes on Your Survey Earnings**

This is often an overlooked issue when it comes to making money from survey companies. While the taxes on your earnings may slightly differ from state to state, you should file your survey income as earnings. This includes gift cards, and any other form of payout from the survey companies.

You should file all of your earnings when it comes to making money with survey websites. It is also good to keep track of all your payments received and to save paystubs. You can keep track of your earnings in the Excel sheet I gave you earlier.

U.S. law requires that market research companies based in the United States must report their payouts to individuals if they payout more than $600 within one year. They will then need to file Form 1099-MISC, and they will need your social security number. **This is the only time it is acceptable to give a market research firm your social security number**.

If you keep track of your earnings, you should be aware which companies would need to file Form 1099-MISC for you. Since taxes differ in every state, I recommend consulting an accountant or other professional advisor to assist you with filing your taxes. I am not a professional when it comes to taxes, I am simply trying to give you some base information to work off and be aware of.

If you live outside of the United States, you should look into your specific tax reporting requirements.

**The Right Mindset to Make the Most Money**

When it comes to taking surveys online, the first thing you should know is that it is not a get rich quick scheme. You won't be able to quit your day job, no matter how much effort you put in.

However, it is more likely that you could make enough to pay for your groceries each month, pay off your car payments, or make enough to have a good chunk of spending money. If you go about it with the right strategy, then taking surveys for money is worth the time and effort when it comes to the payout. Especially when you consider that it is all from your computer, you don't need any qualifications and you can **start earning money right away**.

If you want to make the most money with online surveys, you need to have the right mindset going into it. By this, I mean that you need to think of the long term. Don't think about how much you are making right now, or how much you made in a few days. You should be looking at what you are making at the end of the month and over the course of a year.

I believe in this mindset, because a lot of the features on these survey websites payout small amounts. But it is the small amounts gained consistently over time that ends up with the **bigger paychecks at the end of the month.**

If you only want to make money really quick and be over with it, then you are not taking advantage of the best features of some of these websites. For example, Swagbucks has multiple bonus features, and while they don't seem impressive alone and on a short-term basis, if you take advantage of them, you can add a good amount to your earnings by the end of the month.

Remember, to make the most money with online surveys, you need to think longer term and realize that it is the little things that will add up to the bigger paychecks that can pay for your groceries or help with the car payments.

With the right mindset, and the general survey taking tips, you are already on the path to success with making money online with survey companies. Now, let's get into the best part of this eBook: which survey sites are the best, and how to best use them to make the most money for the least amount of time.

If you're more interested in other opportunities to earn money online, then please try reading my other Kindle book on **How to Make Money as an Amazon Associate**. I've personally made over **$100,000 in commissions as an affiliate,** and several years ago, I even **sold my top Amazon website in a deal worth six figures.**

|  | Items Shipped | Revenue | Advertising Fees |
|---|---|---|---|
| Total Amazon.com Items Shipped | 9915 | $1,281,337.31 | $82,071.22 |
| Total Third Party Items Shipped | 6114 | $378,989.35 | $22,565.37 |
| **Total Items Shipped** | **16029** | **$1,660,326.66** | **$104,636.59** |
| **Total Items Returned** | **-246** | **-$46,689.23** | **-$2,239.44** |
| **Total Refunds** | **0** | **$0.00** | **$0.00** |
| TOTAL ADVERTISING FEES | 15783 | $1,613,637.43 | $102,397.15 |

You can get that Kindle book here:

http://ChrisGuthrieBooks.com/amazon

# The Best Survey Sites and How to Use Them

These sites are the best sites on the Internet to make money with. They are scam free, offer above average payouts on at least one activity, and offer payouts in cash. I will first tell you the individual strengths of each website, but the next chapter will be about **how to combine them all for the most productive money making possible**.

**Important Note:** Every single one of these companies has an affiliate program where I could be compensated if you signed up to join them, but **I'm not using any affiliate links inside this book**.

I just want to be clear that there is no added incentive on my end when if you follow the schedule and use the sites I recommend. I simply want to share what I've learned **about taking surveys, so you know where I've had the best results**.

# Swagbucks

Swagbucks (SB) is one of my favorite sites to make money online. They offer a ton of ways to make money, which is great news if you are able to utilize the methods correctly. Often times, people don't know about Swagbucks best features and get caught up spending their time on the low paying activities. I'll teach you how to not get trapped by them.

First, I will show you how to make the most money when signing up for Swagbucks. These techniques will **at least double your earnings for a registration you would be doing anyways**. Then I will show you the best way to earn the most Swagbucks everyday, and how these techniques will add up to big bonuses by the end.

### Signing Up For Swagbucks

So the first step for doubling your registration is to sign up for Swagbucks.

Once you have successfully signed up, you will be taken to a screen that asks you to complete your profile, learn how to earn SBs, and discover the rewards you can earn. **Don't do these yet.**

| | | Swag Bucks | Minutes |
|---|---|---|---|
| You've just earned 4 Swag Bucks for signing up! Please check your email to verify your account and get started below. | | | |
| | Complete your profile | 20 | 5 |
| | Learn how you earn | 10 | 2 |
| | Discover your rewards | 2 | 2 |
| | Explore on my own. Take me to the homepage. | | |

### Swagbucks Accelerator and Daily Goal

You want to click on "Take me to the homepage," and activate the Swagbucks Accelerator. You can find the Swagbucks Accelerator at the bottom of the homepage under "Ways to Earn." Next, you will be shown the Accelerator programs available. I recommend getting the Accelerator Plus program.

**Start Doubling Your Swag Bucks Every Month**

Join the Accelerator program to maximize your Swag Bucks. You will double your Swag Bucks earned, up to 1500 SB per month. Score more rewards faster than ever.

| Member | Accelerator | Accelerator Plus |
|---|---|---|
| FREE | $4.99 PER MONTH | $9.99 PER MONTH |
| Match up to **0** Swag Bucks per month | Match up to **700** Swag Bucks per month | Match up to **1500** Swag Bucks per month |

With Swagbucks, each SB is worth about $.01. This means that with the Accelerator Plus program, you are paying about $10 to get your earned SBs doubled up to 1,500 SB. This is **an extra $5 per month simply as a bonus.**

If you are worried about not meeting the requirement, simply use it for the first month, and then go back to the free membership.

The next step is to turn "On" your Daily Goal, which is located in the left sidebar on your dashboard. This feature is a goal that Swagbucks gives you everyday to reach. If you hit your goal, you get a few bonus SBs and a new goal, with an even bigger payout bonus if you hit it.

If you hit your goal a certain number of days in a row, you will begin to get Winning Streaks. If you hit your goal everyday for 31 days, which is doable with the strategies I give, then you will end up with a bonus of at least 700 SBs at the end of the month, **which is an extra $7.**

### Turn on Swagbucks Watch and Swagbucks TV

While watching videos is not the most profitable way to actively make money online, it is a great way to passively make money. On the Swagbucks Dashboard, you can go to the Watch section and turn on a video. The best part is that you can also mute this video and then reopen the Swagbucks dashboard in a separate tab.

The video will continue to run, but you don't hear it and you don't see it. The only thing you have to worry about is going back every few minutes to click on a new video. You only earn SBs from watching multiple videos, but if you turn on Swagbucks Watch every time you get on your computer, then it makes a difference.

Swagbucks Watch will add up in the long run. Especially when you consider that you can **earn up to 150 SBs a day through Swagbucks Watch**. That is enough to hit your Daily Goal alone. 150 SBs everyday for an average month of 30 days, is about **$45**.

You can do the same strategy on your smartphone or iPod Touch with their Swagbucks TV app.

With these video features, **you can earn SBs passively while you actively earn SBs in other ways, or even use other survey sites to make money.**

Also, Swagbucks usually has the latest movie trailers available to watch or good cooking videos to check out. So if you are going to search for a video, you should check Swagbucks Watch or SBTV first.

**Finish Setting Up Your Swagbucks Account**

After you have set up all the bonus features and are now passively earning Swagbucks through Watch and SBTV, you can fill out the registration and profile surveys.

First, go into "My Account" and upload a profile picture. After that, go to the "Answer" tab on the top menu and click on "Paid Surveys." This will take you to a page where you can fill out a profile and register for surveys.

**Targeted Email Surveys**
Receive targeted surveys tailored just for you right in your email. Sign up today and fill out your profiles worth 32 Swag Bucks and start earning!

Sign up

**Gold Surveys**
You have the power to influence your favorite brands and earn Swag Bucks at the same time. Take highly targeted surveys and start earning even more Swag Bucks!

Go Now

**Daily Surveys**
Every day you complete a survey valued at 60 Swag Bucks!

Go Now

**Survey Profiles**
Receive highly targeted survey opportunities by filling out your profiles and earn 32 Swag Bucks at the same time

Go Now

Now you will want to add the Swagbucks toolbar to your browser. If you use Google Chrome, it comes in the form of an extension. You get 5 SBs for installing it and 1SB everyday just for having it. I'll talk more about how to use the toolbar soon.

### Swagbucks TV, Watch, and Search

First, you should always remember to turn on SBTV and Swagbucks Watch when you get on your computer. Next, you should **develop the habit of only searching through Swagbucks Search**, which is located in the Swagbucks toolbar/extension. This allows you to get paid for doing something that you would have been doing anyways.

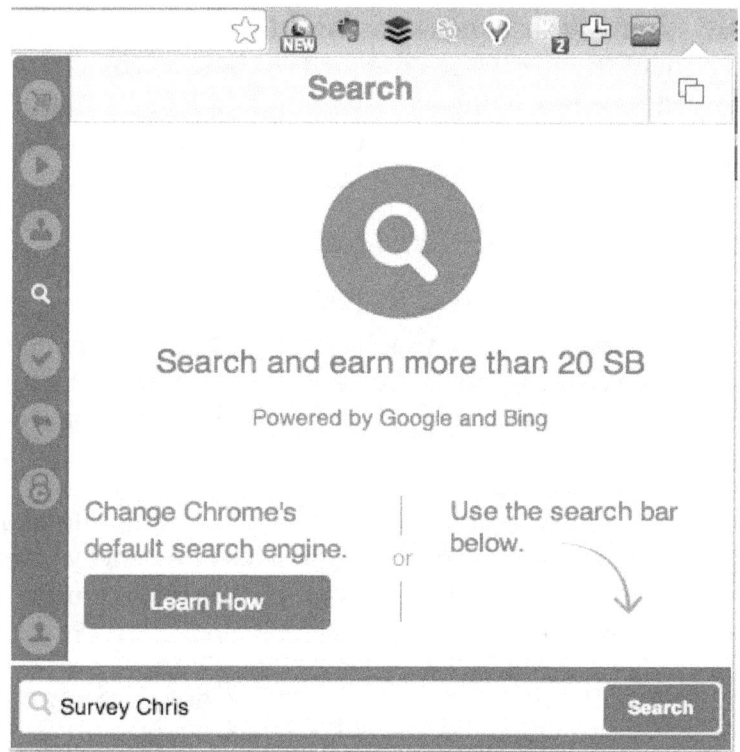

## Swagbucks Daily Poll, NOSO, Surveys, and Paid Offers

Everyday you get a new Daily Poll and NOSO. You should do these everyday. Combined, they only earn you 3 SBs, but will take you about a minute to finish.

Next, you should check your Swagbucks Inbox and see if there are any high paying surveys or offers that they have sent to you. If there are good ones, then I do those first.

After doing the good surveys and offers sent to me, I search through their offers section. Offers are one of **the highest paying ways to make money online**. The reason for this is because they are slightly riskier.

When it comes to paid offers, you need to do some simple math to make sure you are coming out on top. For example, I signed up for a service that cost $5, but I got 880 SBs in return. With using Last Pass, **it took me less than 30 seconds to complete this offer and make $3.80.**

I always make sure to **set a reminder in my calendar and phone to cancel these offers a day or two before the reoccurring charge would happen**, along with keeping track of my earnings and taking notes in the Excel sheet I have shared with you. This way, I make sure that I am always coming out on top.

### Extra Ways to Earn Swagbucks

Other ways you can earn Swagbucks everyday include Swagbucks Codes, which are random strings of letters that Swagbucks publishes somewhere online one to two times a day. Your toolbar or app will tell you where to find the codes, and then you simply copy and paste them into the form to redeem them.

You should also be checking the Swagbucks mobile app while you are out of the house. There are local tasks and surveys that use your location. These can **earn you SBs for running errands or doing things you would be doing anyways.**

Lastly are Swagbucks Coupons and Swagbucks Shopping. Swagbucks offers 10 SBs every time you use one of their coupons, which you can print off from their site. Swagbucks will also pay you to shop online through them. So if you plan on buying something either at the store or online, check with Swagbucks to see if there is a coupon for it, or if you can get it through their online shopping portal.

# CashCrate

CashCrate is similar to Swagbucks in that there are multiple ways to earn money with them. However, CashCrate does not offer the same bonuses as Swagbucks, so there are fewer tricks that you can use to make extra money.

However, CashCrate is still one of my favorite websites for making money because **they also have an offers section**. This is how I make the majority of my money on CashCrate.

They have two sections: one is "Offers" and the other is "Bonus Offers." Make sure you are looking through both of these before filling out any offer, because sometimes the same offer is listed in one section for more than it is listed in the other section.

When it comes to offers, make sure you are following the same rules as I mentioned for Swagbucks offers. Do that math to make sure you come out on top, and then set up a reminder to cancel the service before you get charged again.

The paid offers usually pay out bigger than the free offers, but they are both good options when it comes to utilizing CashCrate.

When it comes to the other activities that CashCrate will pay you for, I have found that they pay lower than the other sites that I will recommend. This is similar to Swagbucks and why I recommend using multiple sites. It allows you to focus only on what each site is best for. In this case with CashCrate it is purely the offers.

Also, CashCrate has a nice referral program that you can use. So if you are able to get people to sign up from a link that CashCrate gives you, then you can get paid for that.

# iPoll

iPoll, which was originally SurveyHead, is one of the websites that I recommend when it comes to completing surveys and tasks. They also have one of the best mobile apps, so that's why it is a top site for me.

iPoll also offers you **$5 just for signing up**, which is a very nice bonus. Once you sign up for iPoll, make sure to fill out the profile questions. iPoll even pays you $.10-$.25 for each profile survey you fill out.

For iPoll, I made sure to fill out the profile surveys first, which helped me qualify for about 75% of the surveys offered. This is a good percentage, but it will vary depending on your demographic. iPoll also **pays above the industry standard for taking surveys**, which is probably the best reason to use them.

iPoll emails you 5-6 surveys a month, which is about the standard with good survey sites. However, iPoll is also good about keeping your dashboard within their website full of surveys for you to take. The access to a lot of surveys, plus their mobile app, makes them a good survey panel to join.

One downside to iPoll is their cash out minimum is $50, which I mentioned earlier. Also, they have to review all their survey payouts before approving them. This means that it will take you longer to get your money with iPoll than it would with other companies.

Why this doesn't bother me is because overall, they are a good survey panel, and I am always thinking longer term when it comes to online surveys by using multiple survey companies. So while I may not get paid out quickly from iPoll, I have checks coming in from other survey companies as well.

## Ipsos i-Say

Ipsos i-Say is another one of the purely survey taking websites that I really like. They pay higher than normal when it comes to surveys, and they have a lot available to you. Overall, **my survey qualification rate was right around 80%**, which was really high.

i-Say offers you a large amount of surveys through the dashboard and through your email. However, sometimes the ones you get emailed will not tell you the payout and the time estimated, so **make sure to skip those**.

They also have a mobile app. However, it is by invitation only, and as of now, I have not been invited, so I cannot speak to it. But one awesome feature that they have similar to Swagbucks is a loyalty program.

This loyalty program gives you bonuses for completing certain amounts of surveys within one year. Starting at 5 completed surveys, you get a bonus of 25 points. Each point is worth about $.01.

If you reach 200 surveys within one year, which is only 4 surveys a week, then you get 2,425 bonus points, **which is about $24.25**. Not the biggest bonus when comparing to Swagbucks $13 monthly bonus, but a bonus is free money, so it's hard to complain.

| N° of surveys | Bonus loyalty points |
|---|---|
| 5 | 25 |
| 10 | 50 |
| 25 | 100 |
| 50 | 200 |
| 75 | 250 |
| 100 | 300 |
| 125 | 400 |
| 150 | 500 |
| 200 | 600 |

When it comes to cashing out with i-Say, you can cash out as early as 1,000 points for $10 with gift cards to Amazon, iTunes and a few other places. The minimum for PayPal is 1,500 points for $15.

However, the best value is to hold out for the $100 PayPal option. The reason for this is because it only costs 9,600. This means **you are saving $4 every time you cash out**. This cash out option, combined with the loyalty program, means that the longer you use i-Say and wait to cash out, the more money you make for your time spent.

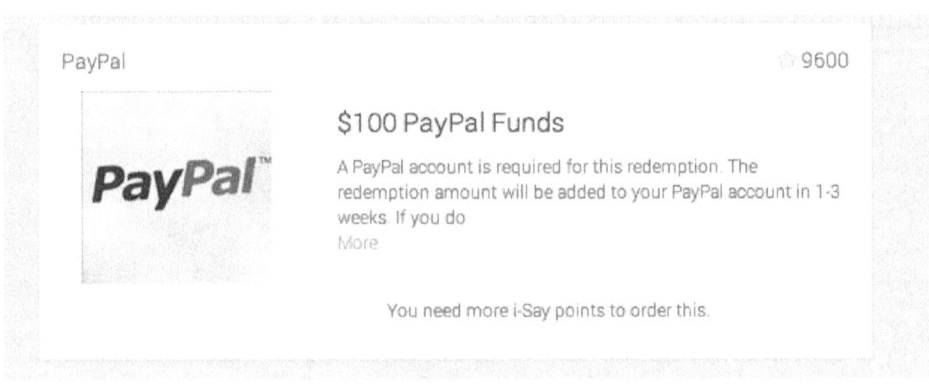

## Opinion Outpost

Opinion Outpost is a survey only website, and they are one of the best. The reason I like Opinion Outpost is because they have a **low payout minimum of $10 via PayPal, and they give it to you instantly**. This is one of the only websites I have come across where you can get paid instantly, which is nice when you have to wait longer for i-Say and iPoll.

The best way to make money with Opinion Outpost is to only take the surveys that you are emailed, since the surveys in the dashboard do not show you how much the payout is and how long it will take.

Luckily, I was getting almost 2 surveys a day emailed to me, and **I qualified at about an 80% rate for them**. Another plus was that when I did get screened out, it never took less than 90 seconds.

Opinion Outpost is another site that works on a point system. However, unlike the other sites, 1 "Opinion Point" equals $.10. This combined with getting surveys that range from 5 to 30 points means that surveys on average pay $.50 to $3, which is pretty good.

I also try to stick with the surveys that only pay 15 points or more, as I have found that those were the ones that I usually finished faster than the estimated time. This means more money for less time spent.

# SurveySpot

Survey Spot is a sister site of Opinion Outpost, as they are both owned by Survey Sampling International. All the tips that I talked about for Opinion Outpost are just as true for SurveySpot.

The only difference is that SurveySpot works on a point system where one point equals $.01. This doesn't really matter because SurveySpot's surveys typically pay out in the 50 to 300 point range, so it ends up being equal with Opinion Outpost.

The only thing you may need to worry about is that you may complete a survey on Opinion Outpost, then go into SurveySpot and click on a survey to realize that it was the same one as the Opinion Outpost survey. They will screen you out of this survey, which is a little annoying.

However, since both survey panels are high paying, I see it as more of a good thing by having two of them. I prefer to focus on one, and then move to the other one once I run out of surveys.

# Paid Viewpoint

Paid Viewpoint is a survey site that seems like a waste of time at first. You get about 1 survey a day, and it typically only pays $.10 to $.20. However, you need to know how Paid Viewpoint works in order to see it's true value.

Paid Viewpoint doesn't only give you money for filling out surveys, but they also give you a "TraitScore." Your TraitScore is a measurement of how much Paid Viewpoint knows about you based on the surveys you have taken for them.

The higher your TraitScore and the more specific of a demographic you are, the more Paid Viewpoint will pay you to answer surveys. This means that while your payout in Paid Viewpoint starts small, if you use it consistently for a long period of time, it can become **one of your highest paying survey panels**.

Also, their website is very nicely designed, and their surveys are some of the shortest and most interesting I have come across, which is always good. Along with those positive aspects, they also have a referral program where you can earn **20% of every person's earnings that you have invited**.

# MindSwarms

MindSwarms is different than the other sites I have listed in that you participate in studies over your webcam. The best part is that **each study takes about 20 minutes and pays $50 within 24 hours.**

While this is an awesome payout for a minimal amount of time, you should know it is difficult to get into the studies. Unlike the other sites I have listed, there is not an endless supply of studies for you to participate in.

They have a section on their website called "Studies for You," where you go and fill out a 5 question application, which then gets sent to the company that has requested the study. They either accept or reject your application, and you are notified within 24 hours.

Since MindSwarms is such a high paying company for such a small amount of work, I recommend applying for every study possible and checking in everyday to see if there are new studies to apply for. You can check in the dashboard or set it up to get emailed every time there is a new one available.

To help you qualify for more studies, you want to record the best sample video of yourself possible. In this video, you want to have high quality video and audio, be very expressive, and give very good descriptions, stories, and details. You can re-record your sample video as many times as you want.

The better your sample video and the more you check in and fill out applications, the better your chances **of getting paid $50 for 20 minutes of work!**

# InboxDollars

Overall, InboxDollars is not one of the highest paying services out there. They offer a lot of activities, like Swagbucks, but I definitely would spend my time on Swagbucks. I include them only for one reason, and that is their partnership with Groupon.

I really like Groupons. Whenever I go out to eat or am looking for an activity to do around town, I check Groupon first, since it is such a great way to save money. If you buy through Groupon, you get $.50 back if the purchase is under $20, but **you get $5 back if it is over $20.**

$5 back on a $20 purchase is a great deal. Especially when you consider that most Groupons save you about 50%. Taking advantage of this is an example of **getting paid for doing something that I would have been doing anyways.**

# BzzAgent

BzzAgent is extremely different from the other websites, but I thought I would include it in case you want to make a little bit of money and **get free stuff**.

BzzAgent is a product testing and marketing firm. The way it works is that once you sign up, you begin filling out surveys. These surveys are used to narrow down your demographic and make you more likely to be accepted to "BzzCampaigns." These BzzCampaigns are product testing campaigns.

**BzzAgent sends you something for free**, which can be anything from a museum tour, to a game console, to a coupon to get a free food product, and many others. You then do the activities that they ask, such as submitting a review or photo, or talking about the product on social media.

Your reviews could be good or bad, but they should be honest. This is how BzzAgent gets its feedback for market research. Not only do you get to keep these products, you also get paid MyPoints for participating. MyPoints can be redeemed at MyPoints.com for a variety of options, such as PayPal or gift cards.

# How to Best Combine all the Survey Companies

While just knowing all the best ways to use these sites is plenty to get you going towards your first $1,000 in surveys, I want to share with you the ultimate way to combine all these sites to **get the most money for your time**. Following this plan will help you earn more money in less time.

Although this will be laid out as a rigid schedule, you should do whatever matches the time and effort you would like to put forth. This is meant to show you the best way to make the most money, but also is adaptable to how you would like to work, whether that is in one big chunk, or smaller chunks of time throughout the day.

This schedule is also assuming that you are already signed up for the sites, have properly filled out the profile surveys (or sample video, in the case of MindSwarms), and are receiving emails from them.

Also, make sure you have Last Pass or Roboform set up to streamline filling out usernames and passwords, along with signing up for offers.

### When First Getting on Your Computer

When you first sit down to your computer, you should immediately open up SBTV on your smartphone or iPod Touch and begin playing videos.

Next you will want to open up your Excel document that I provided to continue to keep track of your surveys and rewards.

After that, open up your Internet browser and use your Swagbucks Search to go to Swagbucks.com and turn on Swagbucks Watch. Make sure to **always use Swagbucks Search to go to new sites.**

### The First Things to Check For: MindSwarms & BzzAgent

The next thing that you should do is head over to your personal survey email inbox. In here you should search for emails from MindSwarms and BzzAgent, since they are the hardest studies to be apart of, so you want to be on top of them.

If you are accepted to either one, make sure to join it as quickly as possible, since they fill up fast. Complete as many steps on those as possible right away, which is different for each company.

### Next is Swagbucks

Since Swagbucks is one of the highest paying sites and hitting the daily goal is important, I do that next. I begin with searching my personal inbox for good surveys and offers from them and do those first.

Then I go to Swagbucks.com, and access my inbox on their website. I search this inbox for good offers or surveys. Sometimes they are the same as the ones I get emailed, but it is still important to check.

After doing that, I do the Daily Poll and NOSO. Then it is time to look for offers. I search the entire site for offers and fill out as many as possible.

Once I am satisfied I have done all of the best offers, but am unsure I will hit the Daily Goal or am really close to hitting the 2$^{nd}$ or 3$^{rd}$ Daily Goal, I will do the surveys within Swagbucks.

Remember to hit the Daily Goal every single day for the biggest payout. **It is as simple as leaving SBTV open on your phone**.

### Time for CashCrate

Since offers are high on my list of favorite ways to make money with these sites, I head over to CashCrate and fill out all the good offers that they have listed. Make sure to check both the "Offers" and "Bonus Offers".

### Now Onto Surveys

Next, I will head back over to my personal survey email inbox (I close it when leaving it first, then use Swagbucks search to head back to it. It only adds a couple seconds and may payout).

In the inbox, I search for surveys from Opinion Outpost, SurveySpot, Paid Viewpoint and iPoll in that order. The order doesn't really matter, except for that I like to work on Opinion Outpost before

SurveySpot and work from the survey companies that send less frequently to those that send more frequently.

After completing all the emails sent to my personal inbox, I head to i-Say.com and then iPoll.com and do all of the surveys possible in their dashboards. Since there are so many available, this is usually how I finish out my schedule for making money with these online sites.

**Always be Earning**

With that being a daily schedule to make the most money with these sites, I am always checking for more ways to earn with these sites.

**Mobile Apps**

Whenever you are away from your computer, have your phone with you, and find a few spare minutes, **you can always be trying to earn with the iPoll and Swagbucks Mobile Apps**. There maybe surveys available for you to do while you wait.

**Local Tasks, Swagbuck Coupons and InboxDollar Groupons.**

If you are leaving the house for any reasons, such as to go to the store, go to a movie, or going out to dinner, you should **check iPoll and Swagbucks mobile apps for local tasks** to see if there is something simple for you to do to earn money.

Before going shopping, compare your shopping list to the coupons available in the Swagbucks Coupon section. **You could get a discount, along with getting Swagbucks in return**.

Like I mentioned before with Groupons, they are great for restaurants and doing fun activities, so there is no reason you shouldn't be using them and, thanks to Inbox Dollars, **getting money back on your purchases**.

**Online Shopping**

If you plan on buying something online, then you should definitely be checking for it first through Swagbucks, InboxDollars, or

MyPoints.com, which is what you'll be using to redeem your BzzAgent points.

With these options, it simply makes sense to get money back for buying something you would already be purchasing.

### Getting Better With Time

The best part about this schedule and the combination of sites is that you will end up **making money more in even less time the more you do it**. For example, with Swagbucks, the combination of the Accelerator, Daily Goal, and Winning Streaks means bigger bonuses the more you use it.

With i-Say, the loyalty program and holding out for the $100 PayPal payout means more money in the long run. The more you use MindSwarms and BzzAgent, the more you will get invited to campaigns. The more you do with Paid Viewpoint, the higher your TraitScore will become, and the more money you'll make with them.

Combine this with the little things adding up, such as the Swagbucks Toolbar or the iPoll mobile tasks, and you will definitely be taking full advantage of these sites. Remember, making money with these sites should be with a long-term mentality. With that mindset, you'll end up **making more money for less time**.

# Final Impressions On Taking Surveys For Money

Making money with surveys is just one of dozens of different methods I've personally made money online with. I routinely write new books based on my experiences, which you can find by visiting ChrisGuthrieBooks.com. As I mentioned before in this book, surveys are obviously not the most profitable method of making money online, but they are incredibly easy to do, and anyone can do them with zero online experience. If you're looking for more ideas on how to make money online, then be sure to check out my blog: EntrepreneurBoost.com

# Thank You

Thank you again for purchasing my book, it means a lot to me that you chose to read my book, and I hope it exceeded your expectations. I focus on writing about topics that I've had substantial personal experience with – and most importantly – success. You won't read theory from me without seeing real examples as well. I focus on learning new things, growing my business, and teaching others how to do the same.

If you enjoyed what you've read, then I would love your help!

Please leave a review for this book on Amazon:

http://ChrisGuthrieBooks.com/reviewbook3

This feedback helps me to stay motivated and continue writing Kindle books that you can use to start or grow your online business. So, if you loved it, please review it!

To your success,

Chris Guthrie

My Blog: EntreprenuerBoost.com

My Email: EntrepreneurBoost.com/contact

My Kindle Books: ChrisGuthrieBooks.com

P.S. Don't forget to get your free bonus list of over 50+ legit survey websites as well. The fastest way to your first $1,000 taking surveys is to sign up for multiple companies:

**Here is my list of over 50+ legitimate survey websites**:

http://ChrisGuthrieBooks.com/bonus-websites

Thank you again.

www.ingramcontent.com/pod-product-compliance
Lightning Source LLC
Chambersburg PA
CBHW070715180526
45167CB00004B/1480